AVRIL LAVIGNE

THE UNOFFICIAL BOOK

Joe Thorley

First published in Great Britain in 2003 by
Virgin Books Ltd, Thames Wharf Studios
Rainville Road, London W6 9HA

A catalogue record for this book is available from the
British Library.

ISBN 1 85227 049 7

Designed by Smith & Gilmour, London
Printed and bound in Great Britain by The Bath Press, CPI Group

Photographs: **StarFile:** reverse front end paper, 2–3, reverse
back end paper (Clyde), 58 (Jeffrey Mayer), 66 (Gene Young);
Retna Ltd: 4, 14–15, 28(L), 28(R), 29, 30–31, 54 (Statia Molewski),
24, 38 (James Patrick Cooper), 32 (Bob Mussell), 35 (J. Scott Wynn),
68, 72–73, 78 (Joe Fornabaio), 42, 47; **LFI:** 6 (Michael Williams/UWIL),
34–35, 40–41, 77 (David Fisher/DF), 37, 39 (Gilbert Flores/CPS),
50–51, 70–71 (John Marshall/JMA), 60 (Jen Lowery/ULOW);
Redferns: 8, 62, 80 (Stockpop.com), 16, 22, 48, 74 (Amanda
Edwards), 20–21, 58–59 (James Emmett), 27 (Stuart Mostyn);
Rex Features: 10–11 (Action Press), 18, 22–23, 56–57, 64–65
(Brian Rasic), 61 (Richard Young), 26–27 (Sipa Press), 52–53
(Erik C. Pendzich), 71 (John Alex Maguire), 45, 46, 66–67, 76–77;
Famous: 13 (Hubert Boesl)

CONTENTS

INTRODUCTION:
BANG GOES POP

Avril Lavigne is a breath of fresh air in a world being suffocated by manufactured pop.

Pop music has developed a stranglehold on the world's charts. But not everyone wants to listen to it. And there are plenty of alternatives, such as nu-metal favourites Limp Bizkit and rock revivalists The Strokes.

At the same time, televised talent contests have developed into a massive phenomenon. For decades, wannabe pop stars have put themselves in front of the unforgiving lens of the studio camera, desperately hoping that being beamed into the living rooms of millions of people will transform their lives overnight. For a very select few it has done. The most obvious examples in the UK are Will Young and Gareth Gates, the cream of the crop of the hugely successful show, *Pop Idol*, and, in the USA, *American Idol*'s Kelly Clarkson. Others were not so fortunate – original UK *PopStars* winners Hear'Say crashed and burned within just eighteen months.

Canadian skate-punk tomboy with attitude and anger... the world fell for Avril Lavigne

Alongside this, bands like the Backstreet Boys and 'N Sync, and artists including Britney Spears and Christina Aguilera, have dominated the charts with slick, polished pop music. Inevitably however, so much sugary pop began to leave a bitter aftertaste in the mouth. People became bored of the repetitive sounds, tired of the formulaic songs that were written by an élite clique of a dozen or so top professional songwriters. There was a groundswell among the younger, music-loving public that yearned for something more genuine, with greater integrity. Pop acts' record sales began to slide markedly as the public scoured the world for their next obsession.

They found it in a gifted teenage girl, a diminutive Canadian skate-punk tomboy with attitude and anger, a bagful of great songs and a lifestyle to match. It was love at first sight. The world fell for Avril Lavigne.

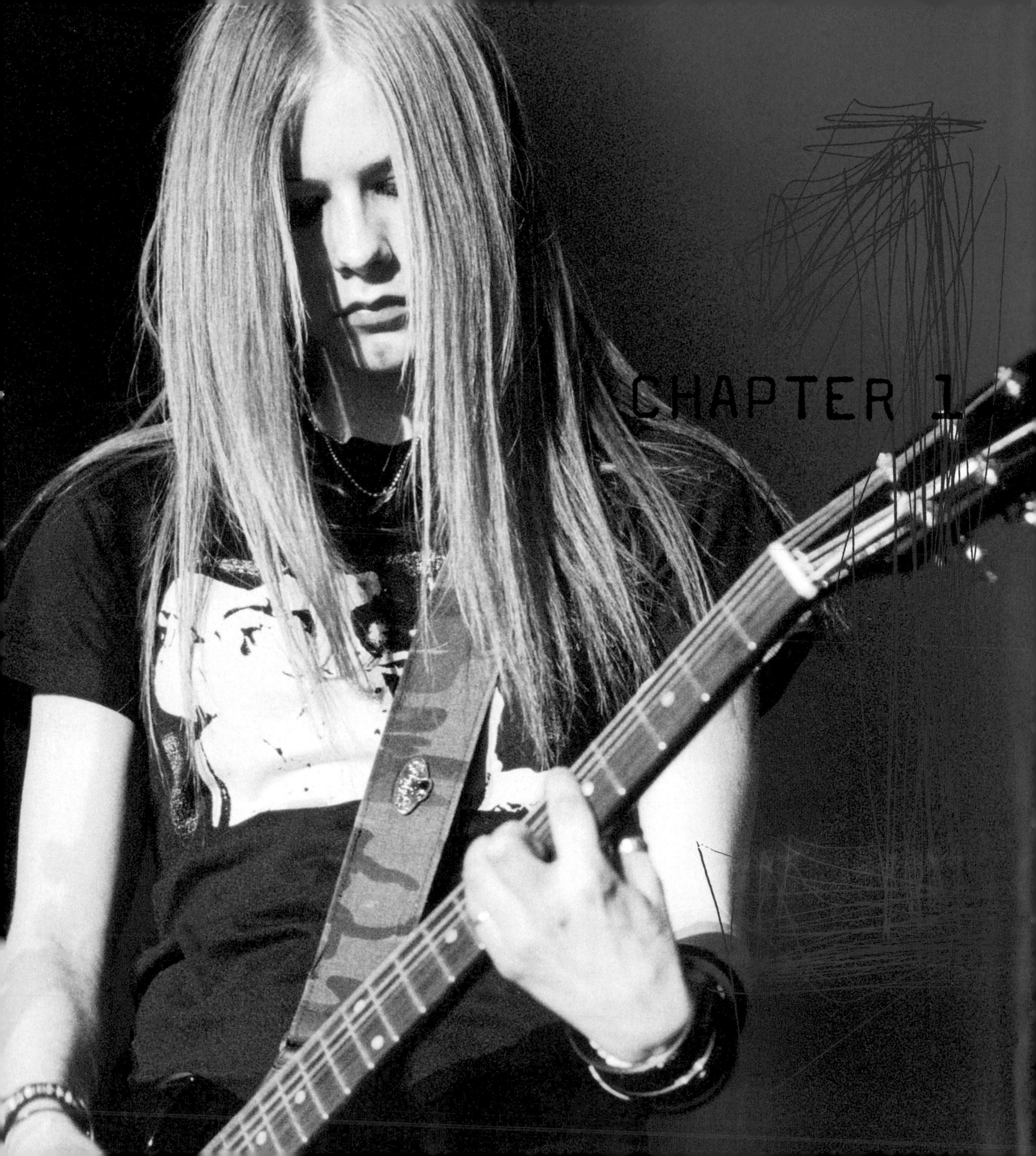

CHAPTER 1

CHICKEN-FRIED CHILDHOOD

Much has been made of Avril Lavigne's small-town childhood. She was brought up in Napanee, Ontario, located halfway between Trenton and Kingston, near the shore of Lake Ontario. The town had less than five thousand inhabitants, hardly a thriving metropolis for a future rock star's formative years. The surrounding environs also offered little excitement for inquisitive teenagers, with Toronto being a full three-hour drive away.

Avril was born on 27 September 1984. The Lavignes moved to Napanee when Avril was just five, relocating from Belleville, Ontario. Avril is the middle child of three, with an older brother, Matt (two years her senior) and a younger sister, Michelle (three years her junior). The Lavigne family home was comfortable, so Avril didn't get into music because of a ghetto childhood.

9

Avril believes she was born 'with music in my blood'

Napanee, with its neat streets and tidy houses, is hardly South Central LA. Like many small outposts in rural Canada, country music is the staple diet of most locals, while the US sports of baseball, football and hockey are also sacrosanct. The modest town is home to a stable and a predominantly farming community, complemented by a smattering of successful career professionals. An unlikely home for a young rock rebel?

Avril's devout Baptist parents, full-time mother Judy and phone company worker father John, quickly submerged themselves in the local church community, primarily at the Evangel Temple. Avril's early experiences of music came from a combination of church and country through her parents. Rebellious? Not really.

Like many female stars before her (Christina, Shakira, Britney and Whitney for example), Avril's first experience of singing in public came through her local church choir. Although she had been singing at home since the age of two, always belting out country songs around the house and in her bedroom, performing twice a week in the church was an excellent way for the youngster to start improving. By the age of ten, Avril was sufficiently accomplished to perform a solo cantata, 'Near to the Heart of God', for the Christmas celebrations. 'She hogged the mike,' recalls her father John. 'She had such a big voice.' Her mother christened Avril 'my little songbird'.

The following year, Avril began borrowing her father's acoustic guitar and eventually persuaded her parents to buy her a six-string of her own. She started teaching herself to play, spending

THERE WAS NOTHING TO DO, SO I HAD TO ENTERTAIN MYSELF. I SPENT A LOT OF TIME WRITING

hour after hour ensconced in her bedroom, forcing tiny fingers into difficult chord shapes. For months she practised Lenny Kravitz's 'Fly Away' over and over and over again. That girl's fingers were sore.

Gradually, Avril decided she wanted to write her own songs, believing she was born 'with music in my blood'. Opportunities to release these growing creative urges were obviously limited in Napanee, but Avril eagerly rooted out what few chances there were to practise or perform. At the age of eleven, she became a member of the town's Lennox Community Theatre that produced amateur plays and musicals for the local community. Singing in musicals had worked as a superb foundation for many superstars, including several members of 'N Sync and the Backstreet Boys for example, but it was hardly enough to warrant a major record deal just yet.

Avril appeared in two shows and, despite her youth and inexperience, she impressed the theatre's director, Tim Picotte. 'She knew back then what she was going to do,' he says, 'and she just kept plugging away at it. Avril has always had the sparkle, she's got showmanship . . . she's always had that since I've know her.' The insular nature of Avril's hometown was eventually referenced in the song 'My World' from her debut album.

It was at Napanee District Secondary School that Avril really began to evolve into the singer-songwriter of *Let Go* fame. For a start, she was a classic tomboy, not a girly girl. Together with her older brother Matt, Avril often went out camping, fishing or hunting. While girls in her class were worrying about the cheerleading squad and make-up, Avril was learning to skate, hanging out with boys and watching jock sports on TV. She played hockey in an otherwise all-boys team during the autumn/winter seasons and baseball in the summer months. She used to play right wing and centre at ice hockey and even got a trophy for the team's 'Most Valuable Player' two years in succession. At one match, she was in a scuffle with the opposition's goalkeeper, a flare-up that her proud dad captured on home video!

Avril was not a wild child at school. She was remembered by one of her teachers as a 'doe-eyed, friendly, polite and determined young woman'. 'I got suspended from school a couple of times,' recounted Avril in *Smash Hits* magazine, 'and I got kicked out of class – for talking and not doing my homework and throwing shit around the room or something.' When she was grounded, she took the time to write music. 'There was nothing to do, so I had to entertain myself,' she said.

Initially, she would write short stories or mini-books as much as songs, but gradually the focus turned increasingly towards music. By her own admission, the first song she ever wrote was a far cry from the hard-edged rock of her future album. It was a simple ballad called 'Can't Stop Thinking About You' which she later described as a 'cheesy cute' track about a teenage crush. There was no shouting in it at all!

I GOT SUSPENDED FROM SCHOOL A COUPLE OF TIMES

Avril's parents worried about their daughter because she was so small, only five feet tall and very skinny. Hanging out with the boys and shunning the traditional girly obsessions, Avril didn't have a great time at school. 'School gave me an inferiority complex,' she says. 'I never did my work, was always talking, and I failed all my tests because I didn't try.' Even so, she had a largely happy childhood, so where did all the rebellion in her songs come from?

At this early stage, Avril's taste in music was predominantly country: artists such as Faith Hill, the Dixie Chicks, Shania Twain and, especially, Garth Brooks. His multi-platinum selling albums in the 1990s dragged boring old country music towards a new era and subsequently re-ignited America's passion for it. The scene was brought completely into the mainstream by the shocking sales figures of artists like Shania Twain, the veteran Reba McIntyre and the glitzier, pop-inflected Dixie Chicks. Suddenly the music was attracting a whole new generation of much younger and edgier fans. Avril Lavigne was a classic example of this

The first was a rock of her

song she ever wrote
far cry from the hard-edged
future album

broader appeal. Other than new country, brother Matt's Goo Goo Dolls albums were one of the few alternative influences Avril might hear in the family home.

Inevitably, Avril started to look further afield than singing in church and at the local theatre, and thus began to compete in talent contests at the multitude of country fairs and weekend shows that could be found littered around the county in the sunny summer months. At these shows, her performances were always renditions of new country favourites, which went down well with her traditionalist neighbours.

Technically, this was a step up from the naked vocals she was used to using in the choir. Avril had to buy a small sound unit to use for her backing tracks, essentially an overblown karaoke machine. For weeks before each show, Avril would practise in her bedroom to the backing tapes all the time, often supplementing them with increasingly polished accompaniment from her guitar.

Then when the time came, she would trudge off to the fair, set up her equipment and sing a set of three songs or so, to a passing crowd busily demolishing their spare ribs and Budweiser, who didn't exactly go ballistic. Little did they know that within a few years, 10,000 people a night would go mad for this girl.

At such a young age, Avril would not have been able to play many of the over-eighteen venues where so many bands and artists cut their teeth. Consequently, these country fairs provided invaluable experience of playing live, learning to use (very basic) sound equipment and presenting herself to a crowd that might need winning over from the first note. Avril persevered and gradually began to win quite a few competitions, even earning a few hundred dollars in prize money. In 2002, when Avril had become the rock star she aspired to be, many observers commented on the fact her live show seems self-assured beyond her age – this was simply because the young Canadian has been out there singing in the public spotlight for years.

Someone else who had been a professional singer for years before her big break was Shania Twain, funnily enough one of Avril's favourite artists. That fellow Canadian singer's own story could not have been more different to Avril's. In Shania's late teens, both her parents were tragically killed in a car accident and she was left to bring up her two siblings while still trying to keep her dreams of a music career alive and pay the bills. Her hard work paid off finally with the mammoth smash album *Come On Over*. Result!

For Avril, Shania was a big early influence. Imagine her excitement then when she heard of a radio competition that offered the winner the chance to sing alongside Ms Twain on stage! Avril duly entered a tape of herself singing along to a Shania song and crossed her fingers – soon after came the exciting news on the phone that she had won. The prize was a coveted live performance with her fellow Ontarian Shania in front of 20,000 fans crammed in to the Corel Centre, singing the latter's 'What Made You Say That?' After the dream-come-true performance for Avril, she proudly told a clearly impressed Shania that she intended to be 'a famous singer'. Avril still recalls this day with relish, 'It was the biggest rush of my life. I walked out on stage and I was the happiest person in the world.'

IT WAS THE BIGGEST RUSH OF MY LIFE.
I WALKED OUT ON STAGE AND I WAS THE
HAPPIEST PERSON
IN THE WORLD

CHAPTER 2.

NEW COUNTRY, NEW WORLD

By the age of fourteen, Avril was ready for her first experience of the recording studio. It came with her contribution to local folksinger Steve Medd's albums, *Quinte Spirit* (1999) and *My Window To You* (2000). Medd first saw a thirteen-year-old Avril during one of the musicals at the Lennox Community Theatre. At the time, he was planning to self-record his own indie album, and felt that Avril's voice perfectly suited some of his song ideas. He played her samples of his material, which cleverly blended folk and country, and she excitedly agreed to work with him in the studio in nearby Kingston.

19

Remember, this was the very first time Avril had ever walked into a recording studio. It didn't matter one bit as Medd recalled to *The Star* magazine, 'It was absolutely amazing. The cut you hear on my CD is one take. This is a fourteen-year-old girl, never been in a studio, walks in like a professional and nailed it. It completely stunned me.' Medd recorded Avril's vocals on the country-gospel tones of the track 'Touch The Sky'. When he decided to record a follow-up album in tribute to the poet E. Pauline Johnson called *My Window To You*, he again called Avril. This time she contributed vocals to two tracks, namely 'Temple Of Life' and 'Two Rivers' (Avril's dad played bass on some tracks too!).

Medd enthused, 'She had the pieces. All the little nuances that truly good musicians can do with their voices. Dynamics was a big thing. Take a song down real soft and then just belt it out within a few bars.'

Despite her future reputation as a 'wild child', Medd suggests that Avril was always a very focused and driven teenager whose maturity was well ahead of her actual years. '[Avril was] just kind of incredibly positive. She babysat both my kids. They will say to this day that she is the best babysitter we ever had. She is engaging with people. She was a joy to work with. She had a real positive spirit about her.'

In the same town as Medd's studio, an artist manager called Cliff Fabri ran his company RomanLine Entertainment. Fabri had helped secure record deals for Jenifer McLaren and Bomb 32, so he knew how to get new artists signed to major labels. He first saw Avril perform at a small local bookstore. He thought her voice was average and her look wasn't great, but he was taken with her presence and composure for someone so young. Convinced she was a future star, he approached Avril with a view to becoming her manager.

If Avril was going to succeed, it would have to be with her own material

One of the most important aspects of Avril's fledgling career –
and one that would hold her in good stead for the later strenuous
demands of her touring lifestyle – was playing live as often as
possible. Fabri arranged numerous gigs and showcases in and
around the Kingston and Napanee area. The country influence
was still prominent, with Avril's set list occasionally being
complemented by the odd pop number, such as a track by the
chart act Sixpence None The Richer.

At this early stage, it wasn't just Avril's musical tastes that
separated her from her latterday skater-punk persona. Her
look was also drastically different from the style she is famous
for today. Her clothes were nondescript and her hair was in no
particular style at all – apart from an ill-fated and thankfully
short-lived flirtation with braids.

Although Avril was only fifteen, recent pop history had
proved that even kids needed to be professional to launch
a career. At that age, Britney Spears was already primed to
hit an unsuspecting world. Back in Napanee, Avril was just an
unknown wannabe, with no original material of her own and
scant live experience. Would she stand a chance?

Avril shot round to her local record store and starting scouring the racks of alternative music

Fabri also encouraged Avril to continue writing her own material. He was not interested in working with a pop puppet; he was reluctant to promote an artist who was merely a mouthpiece for a behind-the-scenes team of writers and super-producers. This girl was going to do it herself.

Yet she was only fifteen. This might seem a tall order for someone who had as yet barely travelled outside her own state, but it did not daunt her at all. In the privacy of her bedroom, Avril started to refine her initially crude efforts at songwriting. While she busily worked away writing, her live set in public continued to consist of cover versions – for now.

Another element of the masterplan was to record a video of Avril performing live both on stage and in her basement(!) and mail this to prominent figures in the record industry. This mass mail-out tactic is normally a sure-fire route to failure, as record company suits get hundreds of tapes a day. However, Fabri cleverly worked his extensive contacts within the industry and got copies of the promo tape into the hands of numerous key players.

One such executive was Brian Hetherman, formerly at Universal Music, who even travelled to Napanee to meet Avril (she performed Sarah McLachlan's 'Adia', Faith Hill's 'Breathe' and one unknown original song) but didn't offer her a deal. But he was impressed and promptly sent her a package of CDs by way of encouragement. One of these, nu-rockers Blink-182, was the first band aside from the Goo Goo Dolls that Avril had heard that was not strictly from the new country genre. Avril went shopping for more straight away, snapping up albums by bands such as Third Eye Blind and Matchbox 20. Would this change her own music?

Meanwhile, her video demo continued to reap positive feedback. The Vice-President of Nettwerk Records, Mark Jowett, asked to meet Avril. On doing so, he suggested she was a little unsure of her exact musical and stylistic direction. Not yet ready to offer her a record deal but intrigued by what he had seen, he suggested Avril travel to New York to work with some big name writers and producers. New York? Yes, please!

CHAPTER 3.

BIG IDEAS
IN THE BIG APPLE

With Avril's video demo tape doing the rounds of record
company talent scouts, Cliff Fabri took quite a few calls from
labels interested in shaping Avril into a Britney/Christina-style
pop clone. After all, she was young, ambitious, very pretty and
already reasonably experienced on the live circuit. Surely she
was prime fodder for moulding into the next teen sensation?
Think again!

Neither Avril nor Fabri were remotely interested in such ideas.
They were both delighted with the proposal of a trip to New York to
work with elite songwriters. On checking into her accommodation
in Manhattan, Avril immediately knew she was a long, long way
from the confines of Napanee. From her hotel window she could
see some of the seedier parts of the city – it was clear straight
away that she was somewhere completely different. It was a
baptism of fire for this small-town girl in a downtown world.

Among the people Avril met in the city was Peter Zizzo, who
had worked with a clutch of top stars such as Jennifer Lopez,
Céline Dion and Alannah Myles. The idea was for Avril to sing
along to some of Zizzo's songs, learn from his experience and

soak up the atmosphere. However, both Avril and Fabri were adamant that she should actually co-write with the seasoned musician. Admirably, Zizzo agreed and the resultant song, 'Why', was the first serious songwriting achievement for the aspiring young Canadian. In the car home after the brief trip to NY, Avril's demo tape was played on repeat and the effect of this self-penned tune on Avril's confidence was huge – she got such a buzz from hearing her own song on the car stereo that she knew this was what she had to do. As the bright lights of New York faded into the horizon, Avril was certain this would not be the last time she visited that city to write music. She was right – what she couldn't have known was that one of these visits to New York would change her life forever.

That same summer saw the release of the debut album, *Can't Take Me Home,* by a female singer-songwriter who prided herself on her rebelliousness: Pink. The rise and rise of Pink boded well for Avril, as there seemed to be many similarities between their two respective backgrounds: Pink's parents' record collection, most notably Bob Dylan and Don McLean, was her first experience of music (her mother is also named Judy); she started writing her own material aged fourteen; unlike Avril, she performed with two bands as a singer, but like Ms Lavigne a solo career was always her dream; most poignantly, she was 'discovered' by LaFace Records' head honcho, the genuine music biz legend, Antonio 'LA' Reid, who then hooked Pink up with various elite songwriters including She'kspeare, Babyface and 112; Reid would also step back from trying to manipulate Pink into a fabricated pop star, instead letting her fashion her own career, sound and image with multi-platinum-selling consequences. This very same man would very soon arrive in Avril's life with a seismic impact.

For now, while Pink was launching her hugely successful career, Avril was back in quiet old Napanee. Straining at the leash to return to New York to work with more writers, Avril eventually secured a second trip. This time, a talent scout named Ken Krongard who worked at Arista Records saw Avril. Impressed, he was anxious for his boss, LA Reid, to see this talented and unsigned girl in person. He asked Avril if she would return yet again to the city to perform a showcase: well, duh! What do *you* think?

I WASN'T
EVEN
EDUCATED
ON
WHAT A
RECORD
DEAL
WAS ⭐27

She has never experienced stage fright in her

entire life

Another trip, another meeting: Peter Zizzo's studio on the very first day of Avril's third trip to the Big Apple. Avril was told she would need to showcase three songs in front of Reid, one of the music industry's most powerful moguls. When the big day came, Avril was somewhat perplexed by all her advisors reassuring her and telling her not to be nervous when Reid arrived. She had hardly heard of him, aside from what people had mentioned, so her teenage confidence simply allowed no room for apprehension. Avril has since revealed that she has never experienced stage fright in her entire life.

This small and private gig was to be the most important single performance of Avril's life. Yet, remarkably, she openly admitted to being largely unaware of the mechanics of the record business. 'I wasn't even educated on what a record deal was,' she said. 'All I knew was that if I sang for this guy and if he liked me, that would make me be able to get a record and that's all I wanted. I wanted my CD.'

Reid sat in silence and watched Avril perform two Zizzo compositions, plus their collaboration 'Why'. At the end of the mini-set, Reid politely thanked Avril for singing to him and told her she was wonderful. Then he left. He didn't even know that Avril wrote her own songs.

Sitting nervously in Zizzo's studio, Avril was not sure whether the showcase had gone well enough to secure her that dream recording contract. Fortunately, she didn't have to wait long to find out. Shortly after Reid left, a stretch

limousine appeared unannounced at the studio and whisked
Avril and Fabri off to dinner at the top of the twin towers of the
World Trade Center. Reid was there and offered her a record
deal, rumoured to be worth in excess of $1.9 million, on the spot.
Shortly after, Avril was also offered a $1.4 million publishing
advance. That's pretty big.

These figures, if correct, are all the more remarkable when
you think of the weakness of the record industry and the cost
of launching a shiny new act (it is said to cost £1 million to launch
a pop act just in the UK). New record deals are rare; older, less
successful artists are being dropped like stones.

Now, here was an unknown teenager with two contracts on
her manager's desk worth a total of $3.3 million. Fabri had once
predicted that Avril would be a millionaire before she had sold
her first record. He was right. Avril had only just turned sixteen.
Pretty good going.

LA Reid had not just steered the career of Pink to dizzy heights
– he had also played a major role in the success of Toni Braxton,
TLC and Usher. With his portfolio at his own label LaFace being
more renowned for such R'n'B stars, there were a few raised
eyebrows when it was announced that as the President of Arista
he had signed a white, teenage rocker. He saw things much more
simplistically – Avril was a star and that was all he needed to know.

It wasn't just the record deal that was offered to Avril. She was
given access to a plush apartment in New York's Greenwich Village,
historically a haven for artists and creative types. The problem
was that she needed to move to New York full time to record her
debut album, but she was still at school! A big move. 'I wasn't
going to turn it down,' she said about her subsequent decision
to leave school unfinished. 'It's been my dream all my life.'

So picture the scene: deeply religious family – teenage
daughter arrives home, says she's dropping out of school to be
a singer, she's scored a colossal record deal and moving straight
to New York City – you might expect the parents to go mental.

Not so – to their immense credit, John and Judy Lavigne were
unreservedly supportive of Avril's big break. 'They knew how
much I wanted this,' she told one reporter, 'and how much I've

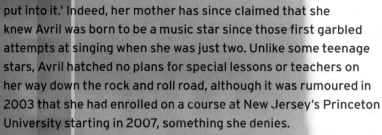

I STARTED WORKING WITH THESE REALLY TALENTED PEOPLE, BUT I JUST WASN'T FEELING IT

put into it.' Indeed, her mother has since claimed that she knew Avril was born to be a music star since those first garbled attempts at singing when she was just two. Unlike some teenage stars, Avril hatched no plans for special lessons or teachers on her way down the rock and roll road, although it was rumoured in 2003 that she had enrolled on a course at New Jersey's Princeton University starting in 2007, something she denies.

Although delighted, Avril's parents were understandably a little apprehensive at their little girl going to work and live in New York. It was therefore decided that her brother Matt would escort her there and live with her while she worked on the record. Matt, who was only in his late teens himself, didn't need to be asked twice to share a luxury apartment while travelling around the music business hot spots of NYC with his sister!

Their apartment was in Horatio Street in the Village, where Avril spent four exhausting months. It was a tough time: she was always moving in circles with people much older than herself and, although she was more than capable of spending day after day in adult company, she craved some interaction with kids her age. What is more, when Matt wasn't around, she was stuck home alone, with just her music for company.

Worse still, it quickly transpired that there were potential differences of opinion about the extent of her contribution to the actual writing on the debut album. Arista remained unaware that she was a developing songwriter and, perhaps naturally, sent her to work on the songs of other more established writers. Perhaps naturally, many of the songs given to her were very much from the 'new country' ilk – a style that had featured heavily in her showcase – and on the surface were perfectly suited to both her voice and musical background.

However, Avril couldn't stand this material, despite trying hard for several weeks to make something gel and feeling increasingly under pressure for results. As she revealed to *Entertainment Tonight*, 'I started working with these really talented people, but I just wasn't feeling it; the songs weren't representative of me. I had to write myself. I had to do my music. It was a really stressful time, but I never considered giving up.'

CHAPTER 4.

NOTHING IS SIMPLE

Over many frustrating months, Avril tried in vain to collaborate with nearly a dozen professional songwriters sent by Arista. With the pressure mounting, she left New York and headed three thousand miles across the United States to Los Angeles, to meet up with yet another renowned songwriter, Clif Magness. Just like all the other writers Avril had tried to work with, Clif had created songs for countless stars, but this liaison was totally different – the two struck up a fantastic chemistry immediately, quickly producing dramatic results. 'I was like, "Yeah! I've found my guy!"' says Avril. 'We totally clicked, because he just let me guide; he really understood me and let me do my thing.' At their very first writing session together, Avril and Clif conceived and completed the future album track 'Unwanted'. Fast work.

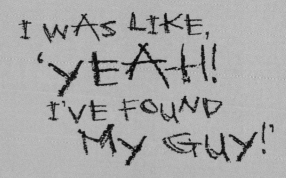

I WAS LIKE, 'YEAH! I'VE FOUND MY GUY!'

Within a few days, the duo had completed several key tracks which would feature on her debut album, including 'Sk8er Boi', 'Losing Grip', 'Unwanted', and 'I'm With You'. Arista had been expecting more countrified material. However, as each day passed and they continued to turn up with tape after tape of high quality rock tracks, the wariness began to fade – eventually they gave in, and pronounced themselves delighted with the LA recording results.

While in Los Angeles, Avril also teamed up with the ultra-trendy production team of The Matrix (husband and wife Lauren Christy and Graham Edwards, plus Scott Spock) who had collaborated with artists such as Christina Aguilera, Backstreet Boys and Liz Phair. This latest partnership added yet another element to the recording sessions.

'It was my favourite time in LA,' Avril says. 'I've never seen orange trees before. I remember sitting in the backyard behind the studio and just freaking out because of the orange trees!' On a more creative level, away from the claustrophobic atmosphere of New York, Avril now found herself able to turn the loneliness she had felt there into an inspiration. 'Being away from home, being on my own and having this new life, I had so much to write about,' she said. Unlike the non-specific pop rants of artists like Britney Spears, these were songs that were very much inspired by Avril's own life experience. 'Once I sit down with the guitar, I write about what I'm feeling that day,' she says. 'I don't usually go,

As each day passed and they continued to turn up with tape after tape of high quality rock tracks

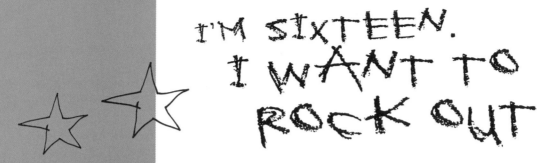

I'M SIXTEEN. I WANT TO ROCK OUT

"I'm going to write a song about this," and then write a song. I just sit down and whatever's in my heart usually just comes out.' She was loving it. 'When I get upset and really need to get it out of me I go to my guitar. Sometimes I feel like my guitar is my therapist.'

Avril, Clif and the Matrix made a great combination. One great example of this productive process came out of Avril's very first meeting with the Matrix team. The three writers had already penned a tentative track in anticipation of Avril's arrival but were saddened to find that neither she nor Fabri liked it. Instead, Avril played them the demo of 'Unwanted' that she had written with Clif Magness in order to offer them some insight into what she was looking for.

Fabri then left the quartet alone in the studio, promising to return some time later that afternoon. 'She came to our studio and the record company was looking for Faith Hill-type songs, but she didn't seem to be into that at all,' recalls The Matrix's Lauren Christy. 'So we said, "What do you want to do?" She said, "I'm sixteen. I want to rock out."' Avril herself recalls, 'Graham sat down with the guitar and was, like, "Listen to this little idea I have," and I was like, "Oh cool," and then me and Lauren started singing to it. And we just recorded the guitar part and then went and laid on a blanket in the sun and wrote lyrics to it, Lauren and I.'

On his return to the studio later that same afternoon, Fabri was amazed to find they had completed this entire song ready for the album – only three takes were needed, no vocal overdubs used and no clever studio wizardry to patch up mistakes. The song's name? 'Complicated'.

Before Avril could prepare to unleash her debut album on an unsuspecting world, there were changes afoot for those around her. Two weeks after the recording of her breakthrough hit 'Complicated', she parted company with Cliff Fabri as her manager and was taken under the wing of the increasingly powerful Nettwerk Management stable, who also boasted big-name clients such as Coldplay, Dido, Barenaked Ladies and Sarah McLachlan.

Avril's album was not recorded entirely in one studio, like many records. The majority of the songs were captured in two principal locations, both in California, namely Decoy Studios in Valley Village (the home of The Matrix) and Blue Iron Gate Studios in Santa Monica (predominantly used by Clif Magness). The recording sessions also saw Avril flit across the country to NYC for 'Nobody's Fool', which was ably produced, arranged and co-written by Peter Zizzo; she also headed to Boulevard Recording Studios in New Jersey for 'Tomorrow' and 'Naked'.

The mixing of the album, when all the songs are perfected and fine tuned by expert ears, was a little less hectic for Avril. Ten of the tracks were mixed at South Beach Studios in Miami by Tom Lord-Alge. Two more ('Naked' and 'Too Much To Ask') sent her back to New Jersey's East Iris studios before the job was finally finished at Henson Studios in Hollywood, California (the sole track that was mixed on the west coast). The whole album was executive produced by Antonio Reid, who is thanked by Avril on the liner notes for allowing her 'to be myself'.

All the songs were co-written by Avril, either with The Matrix and Clif Magness, with Zizzo working on the creation of 'Nobody's

Fool', while the pairing of Curt Frasca and Sabelle Breer combined with Avril for another two tracks ('Tomorrow' and 'Naked'). Considering Avril was so young and relatively inexperienced, this complete involvement in the actual writing of the album was a sizeable achievement. Throughout the sessions, executives from Arista visited the studio and, when repeatedly faced with so many great songs, were constantly amazed to hear that Avril had co-written. That little girl? No way!

The album had taken time to get right, but they had finally got there. 'I just write songs right away,' says Avril. 'I don't spend five million hours on it dissecting it. When I start the lyrics, I just write them all the way through because I feel that way at the moment, so I just get it all out of me. It would be really weird if I spend one [whole] day on it.'

As for a title, it needed to reflect the effort she'd put in. She told one reporter how, 'When I thought about what I did that whole year of writing, I felt like I really let a lot of things go, a lot of stuff off my chest. It's a positive thing for me. I knew that I would soon be in the public eye and having people rip me apart and judge me and good things and bad things would be said about me and I knew that whenever negative stuff came my way, I would just have to like shove it away, let it go.'

Let Go was the title which Avril settled on. The album was pencilled in for release in June 2002. All she had to do now was wait.

In the meantime, Avril had a debut single to release: 'Complicated'. Spontaneous and addictive, the opening gentle acoustic guitar strums and 'la-la-la-la' backing vocals (courtesy of The Matrix) were overlaid by the spoken word whispers about 'life'. This was then segued into a similarly gentle first verse, suggesting less of a rocker child than Avril might ideally prefer. Indeed, in many ways, this was one of the forthcoming album's most lightweight songs, hardly a declaration of punk intent. However, it was a great song nonetheless, a sure-fire radio hit and the perfect showcase for Avril's forthcoming album.

The song is a plea to Avril's boy/friend (it seems unclear which) to just be himself and drop the façade he has adopted to impress people. She mocks his 'preppy clothes', surely a snide jab at the jocks who ignored her in favour of the Barbie-doll look-alikes in her class. She also has a go at his cocky attitude and vain efforts

SOMETIMES I FEEL LIKE MY GUITAR IS MY THERAPIST

to be cool, which instead leave him looking like a fool. But Avril is obviously still fond of him, closing the song by hoping that if only he could 'let it be' and be himself.

'In this past year I've really grown as a writer,' Avril reflected when asked about this single. '"Complicated" wasn't written about anyone in particular. It is basically about life, people being fake and relationships.' Avril's vocal is pushed very high in the mix, almost as if she is talking to you personally, so it is a good job that her voice has so much depth. Altogether, the song is a powerful formula, an impressive debut and was a teaser for the album.

The video for the single was the ideal complement to the song. It showed Avril decked out in skater gear, hanging out with her friends and crashing the local shopping mall. This was a genuine shopping centre which remained open throughout the shoot. At that point, Avril was an unknown so she could do this – if she tried the same trick now, the shopping mall would be besieged by fans!

Despite the song's reference to life's complexities, the video reminded the viewer that most people Avril's age were in fact enjoying a rather simpler life. The clip ended up winning loads of awards, including most notably the MTV award for 'Best New Artist In A Video'.

As with her music, Avril has close input in her videos. At the same time, there is always plenty of spontaneity on the day of the actual shoot! 'They were going to have us driving around in those carts,' she remembers. 'Then we all of a sudden started crashing into stuff. The mall was open and we started bumping into each other and we were all laughing and pissing ourselves.' Although Avril finds promotions a chore, filming videos is something that she definitely gets a kick out of. She says, 'Yeah, videos are fun. It's very cool cause you're the star of the day and everyone's doing your hair and your make-up and taking care of you. It's fun!'

Music television channels adopted the video and song instantly as a heavy rotation favourite, while American and English radio found that the song's innocuous sounds slipped in very nicely among almost any playlist. As a result, the song received huge coverage prior to its early summer 2002 release. The anticipated public interest in this just-be-yourself anthem was high, with stores advance orders suggesting Avril might be heading for a fantastic start to her chart career on both sides of the Atlantic.

'Complicated' debuted high in the *Billboard* charts, but rose to the top slot after eight weeks, staying at number one for several weeks thereafter. The same feat was replicated in her home country, while in the UK she reached number three. Across Europe too, where rock music often takes second place to dance tunes, Avril enjoyed a clutch of number one positions too; even in Australasia she went to the top of the charts. Almost overnight, she was an international star.

With surprising calmness, Avril played down the massive success of her first ever record. 'I didn't ever think about the charts, because I never knew about them until I got into the business. But I did always believe in myself.' Might she have thought about the charts a little more if 'Complicated' had bombed?

The success of the single did not stop there. In 2001, the song 'How You Remind Me' by Canadian rockers Nickelback had broken the world record for most plays on American radio in one single week – an astonishing 9,050 spins! That's nearly one play every minute somewhere in America, 24/7. So imagine the excitement in the Lavigne camp when her management were informed that she had broken that record with a colossal 9,205 spins in a single seven-day spell. Then it was announced that 'Complicated' had enjoyed the most weeks at number one on the Contemporary Hit Radio chart lists, a key indicator of which acts were the hottest in America. The record had previously been held by Madonna's single 'Music' in 2000. North of the border, 'Complicated' was also the most frequently heard song on Canadian radio that year. How big could Avril get with just one song?

Perhaps the oddest trophy the track scooped was 'Best Homework Song' at the Radio Disney Awards

When the end of year industry gongs were dished out, 'Complicated' won a prestigious Canadian Juno Award for 'Single of the Year' as well as the MTV Video Award. Perhaps the oddest trophy the track scooped was 'Best Homework Song' at the Radio Disney Awards! (At the same ceremony she would also win 'Best Female', 'Best Song' and 'Best CD'.) What a way to start your career!

On its release, 'Complicated' saw comparisons being drawn between Avril Lavigne and many established singers. As some critics pointed out, on first listen, Avril does indeed sound like so many female singers before her – Alanis Morissette, Tori Amos, Lisa Loeb, Michelle Branch and Vanessa Carlton for example. Vanessa Carlton had sold more than 500,000 copies of her first album in a few months. Michelle Branch enjoyed even more success with her million-selling *The Spirit Room* – both also had large involvements in the writing of their records. Observers suggested that these two performers had paved the way for singles like 'Complicated' to be accepted by the public and the music industry.

That said, Carlton and Branch may have opened doors for Avril in North America, but their success overseas was much more limited and thus Avril has had to create the opportunities internationally herself. Already, Avril was realising that along with fame and success came media attention, snide comments and bad reviews. It was the start of a love-hate (or should that be hate-hate?) relationship with the press that Avril made no secret of her dislike for.

CHAPTER 5.

GIRL ALOUD

Let Go starts with the clanking, quirky 'Losing Grip'. Avril delves into themes of rejection and betrayal, something that she seems more than happy to make public. The song recounts how Avril finally sees a one-sided relationship for what it is – even suggesting that he might be on the rebound or even that she is a look-alike of a former lover. Her disappointment and sadness is tangible. 'That is definitely [about] one of my ex-boys,' explained Avril in her own press bio. 'He didn't give me what I needed emotionally. It doesn't matter now, and plus I got a good song out of it.' This is said to be Avril's favourite song on the album, hence its pole position on the record. It is likely that this will also be the fourth and final single from the debut album, with a video having been recorded in New York in late February 2003 (fans were invited to be in the studio 'audience' and MTV's *Making The Video* were on hand to capture the shoot).

There are reminders of Dido on this track, but vocally this song is the closest Avril comes to Alanis Morissette, particularly the snarling close to each verse and the crashing chorus lyrics when you can almost see her spitting each word out. In the bridge, the use of a voice-box effect adds to this sense of bitterness. It is hard not to see this track as a sister tune to Alanis's own bitter ode to a resented former love, 'You Oughta Know'.

She openly pines for a stable and steady home life

Next up was the debut single, 'Complicated', now an international smash hit. Keeping the momentum high, future second single 'Sk8er Boi' follows. A collision of guitar riffing, dampened hard rock strumming and thunderous drumming, this was a track that could have equally been at home on a Blink-182 album or a classic early 1980s new wave record. Again, Avril's vocals were noticeably high in the mix, helping to highlight the bountiful and essentially pop melodies, which dance all over the hard rock backing.

Lyrically, the song is perhaps Avril's most narrative effort from *Let Go*, a real short story set to music. The track tells the tale of an ill-fated relationship between a punk boy and ballerina girl, and more particularly how the latter denied her feelings and turned her nose up at him to save face with her snobby friends. This conservative girl who repels from the more edgy 'Sk8er Boi' appears to be as equally preoccupied with impressing people as the boyfriend who Avril chided in 'Complicated'. It transpires in the second verse that he has become a millionaire rock star while she is stuck at home with a young baby. In a neat twist, Avril closes the song by revealing that she and the sk8er boi are an item.

With the references to rock stars and MTV, surely this was about Avril? 'So many people ask me that,' she says with exasperation. 'No, it's not. But it is when you think about it. It totally is.' That clears that up, then! She did clarify this a little by saying, '[It's drawn from] what I went through in high school and what I saw in high school, and how different people acted and treated each other . . . I just kind of took that and put it into a story. I wasn't talking about a certain guy or girl.'

A trio of singles is completed by her third release, 'I'm With You'. This is a beautiful yet powerful ballad, cleverly crafted, slightly quirky in its arrangement and a poignant example of Avril's more sophisticated side. She felt the emotion of this song deeply when recording it. 'I went into the booth to sing it with just so much emotion. I had, like, goose bumps going down my spine. It was really neat. When I sing that song, I just like to stand there in my own world. That is an important song to me.'

Avril sings in sombre mood, perplexed by life, unsure of herself or her lover, clearly feeling all the uncertainty and insecurity of a typical teenager. The instrumentation is very modest, tactfully controlled so as not to suffocate the simplicity of the track. Avril's

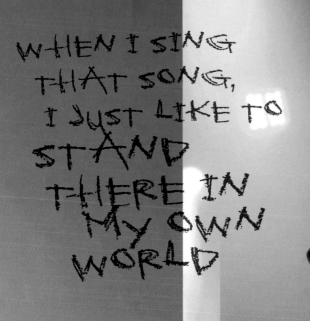

WHEN I SING
THAT SONG,
I JUST LIKE TO
STAND
THERE IN
MY OWN
WORLD

vocal stops the song from degenerating into a clichéd power ballad – her voice uses just the right amount of inflections and detail, all very impressive for a singer of such a tender age.

Then it was back to the jaunty, seductive beats of 'Mobile'. Gentle acoustic strumming underpins the simple beat, but the killer element is Avril's vocal, the way she pronounces her words infectiously, weirdly and yet so clearly. Once more a softer verse crashes into a jarring chorus before falling back into another softer, but equally intriguing verse.

An obvious reference to Avril's transient rock star lifestyle, she openly pines for a stable and steady home life, with regular friends rather than hotel rooms, featureless bathrooms and room service. It seemed a little early in her career to be complaining about the rigours of the road, not least because she had barely been out on the road compared to many artists, but nonetheless at least this musical moan was delivered with a degree of class.

The mixture of exuberance and angst showcased on 'Losing Grip' fails to inspire when it is used again on the album's sixth track, 'Unwanted'. The guitars are too bland, the vocals too predictable, it just feels like formula Avril. Created during her first session with Clif, it fails to hit the spot. Ex-manager Cliff Fabri disagrees: 'When I heard "Unwanted" we were literally doing ring-around-the-rosie. Jumping up and down, high-fiving!' Arista weren't; they were worried it was too rocky.

Fortunately, Avril bounces right back to top form for the next track, the beautiful and seductive 'Tomorrow'. Admittedly straight out of the mould of recent female singer-songwriters, this is a mellow, melodic and magnificent summery stroll. The underlying hint of uncertainty marks out another tale of problematic relationships and the wretchedness of adolescence, the lyrics are largely vague, but this makes no difference as the instrumentation is so enjoyable.

The obviously autobiographical 'Anything But Ordinary' offers the flipside to the impersonal life Avril's been living. This song is an admission that all the demands of touring and being a rock star are worth it if a 'normal' lifestyle is the alternative. Is she saying our lives are too 'normal' for her? Her own record company bio sums this up best. 'I have this awesome opportunity to fulfil my dream,' she says. 'I am all over the place, flying here and there, going through different stuff every day. This is my lifestyle, but I wouldn't want a normal life or I'd get bored.' The phrase 'anything but ordinary' was also used on Avril's official press biography and this has since become her signature song, encapsulating as it does everything that she stands for. It sums up millions of young people's lives perfectly.

The next track, 'Things I'll Never Say', is a reminder of Avril's youth, which accurately captures that awkwardness and self-conscious uncertainty of teenage love. It might be difficult to imagine the cocksure and confident Avril found in magazine interviews could feel like this, but here's the proof: blushing, stumbling over her words and nervously adjusting her clothes whenever this certain boy is around her. She goes so far as to fantasise about their proposal, the wedding and indeed wishes her life away – yet when reality bites she can barely bring herself to speak to him. Lively backing vocals, pure pop sounds of ringing guitar riffs and playful acoustic strums make this track a feel-good anthem.

The pop theme continues with the sunny 'My World'. The lyrics offer a fly-on-the-wall look inside Avril's tomboy childhood and suburban roots, even going so far as to actually mention her hometown. Far from being a rock song, this is breezy, unadulterated pop, but Avril should not be ashamed of this, it is a great tune, a simple song and a credit to the album.

The struggle to get her talents as a songwriter recognised and to avoid being shaped into a pop clone appear well documented in 'Nobody's Fool', through the tale of a controlling boyfriend. The verse's rapping is clumsy and painful, sounding totally out of place, although the song is rescued slightly by the perky and addictive chorus. It's a weak spot on the album.

The penultimate track, 'Too Much To Ask', is a sad muse on an ex-boyfriend. This girl seems to have no luck with men! Delivered through a gentle and subtle series of momentous choruses and tranquil verses, this is another song that seems to be mature beyond Avril's years (by her own admission she had only been in love once, 'It didn't work out'). When cynics suggested this was a sign that the professional songwriters around her may have been more heavily involved, she had the perfect retort, 'I've been through a lot because I'm in the business and it's aged me. I've had to take care of myself and make really important decisions, and I'm around adults 24–7.'

The closing song, 'Naked', uses an almost trip-hop beat mixed with a country and western chorus to tell yet another story of vulnerability. Perhaps the album's first positive love song, Avril admits to her emotional nakedness around this new love, but declares that this can only be a good thing. The song could easily have been written by a middle-aged country singer, but here, when sung by a teenage rock prodigy, it has an equally profound effect. It closes the album on a sophisticated and pensive note. The final track of a healthy thirteen songs (another twenty or so tracks didn't make the cut), this song maintains the ultra-high standards set throughout most of *Let Go*. Avril was excited about what she had achieved, saying, 'It really shows all the different sides of me. I'm a person with a ton of energy who likes to scream and party and rock out. And there are other sides of me that are real serious.'

For an established artist to release such a record was impressive enough – for a girl who was only two years out of high school, it was a positive triumph. Anything but ordinary? That would be a yes.

by her own admission she had only been in love once

CHAPTER 6.

THEY'RE WITH YOU, SK8ER GRRRL

In the USA, *Let Go* charted at number eight on its June 2002 release, selling over 100,000 copies within the first two weeks. That was nothing compared to the amount that would eventually be sold, but it was an excellent start. In Canada, the debut was even higher, at number two. In typical punk style, Avril celebrated her debut in the American top ten album charts by playing a lively gig as the opening act at a tiny club in Hollywood's Sunset Strip. Backed by her live band, she played a rousing seven song set to a mostly music biz crowd which was met with generous applause.

In the UK, the album only managed a top ten placing, but again this was merely the start of a lengthy and progressive campaign that would eventually see the record top the charts on both sides of the Atlantic. The quickest momentum was gained in the USA - platinum status came within five weeks, by which time she was already double platinum in Canada. Within nine weeks, the album had sold one million copies in those two countries, and was also doing hefty business all over Europe, Australasia and the Far East.

The press met the release with strong praise, suggesting that this could herald the arrival of a genuine new talent. Of course, there were some doubters who suggested Avril was little more

By the halfway mark of her performance, almost her entire backside was showing!

than a clever record company creation, but thankfully most writers understood that this was a commendable opening effort. With 'Complicated' still receiving saturation radio and MTV play, sales of the album continued to accelerate.

Just as with that first single, the record books had to be re-written after it was announced that *Let Go* was the first album by a solo artist to see rising sales five weeks in a row in America.

Such quick and sizeable commercial success is rarely coupled with critical acclaim, but here, too, Avril managed to triumph. She was the recipient of five Canadian Radio Music Awards for 'Best New Solo Artist (Rock)', 'Best New Group or Solo Artist', 'Best New Solo Artist', 'Fan's Choice Award' and the 'SOCAN Songwriter Award'. Back at home, Avril won four prestigious Juno Awards for 'Single of the Year' for 'Complicated', 'Pop Album of the Year', 'New Artist of the Year' and 'Album of the Year'. Fittingly, these awards were handed out at the Corel Centre in Ottawa, the very same venue where an aspiring Avril had sung alongside Shania Twain and told the megastar that her ambition was to be a famous singer.

She also scooped three MTV Asia Awards ('Favourite Female Artist', 'Favourite Breakthrough Artist' and 'Style Award'). On the night of the ceremony, Avril flew in especially to perform in front of 8,000 feverish fans at a huge indoor stadium in Singapore, proof positive that she had already become a truly international star.

She has
a point
of view
kids can
identify
with

IF THERE'S ONE AWARD I WANT TO WIN, IT'S FOR THE 'BEST FEMALE ROCK PERFORMANCE'

Most prestigiously of all, she was nominated for an incredible five Grammy awards, placing her alongside other luminaries such as Eminem, Bruce Springsteen, Ashanti and Sheryl Crow. She was tipped for 'Best New Artiste', 'Best Pop Vocal Album', 'Song Of The Year' (for 'Complicated'), 'Best Female Pop Vocal Performance' (for 'Complicated') and 'Best Female Rock Performance' (for second single 'Sk8er Boi'). Her reaction to the news was as you would expect, saying, 'It's great to be nominated for so many awards. But if there's one award I want to win, it's for the "Best Female Rock Performance".'

Unfortunately, on the night of the Grammys, Avril came away empty-handed, although she did get the chance to perform 'Sk8er Boi' in front of two billion TV viewers. She also came away with nothing from the influential Brit Awards in the UK.

At the Muchmusic award ceremony, screaming fans were treated to rather more of Avril than they were used to seeing. Taking to the stage in a particularly low-cut pair of baggies, unbeknown to Avril her heavy microphone pack at the back of her pants started to pull the trousers down. By the halfway mark of her performance, she was practically mooning the audience! 'Do I care?' she asked. 'No! I think it's funny!'

Avril also appeared on the high-profile late-night chat show circuit, on shows such as *Tonight With Jay Leno*. Another publicity coup came when one of her songs was played during the season finale of *Felicity*. As a result, she became one of 2002's most prominent new stars. Everywhere you turned you would either hear an Avril song, an interview on the television or in a magazine. In restaurants, on the radio, in bars, at train stations – there was no escape!

Over the next six months, with all this coverage and another two singles, *Let Go* started to notch up sales that no one within Arista or Avril's empire could have dreamt of. 'She's a great singer and songwriter,' commented a delighted LA Reid. 'She has a relevancy to people her age. She has a point of view kids can identify with.' By Christmas 2002, the debut record had achieved sales of a staggering ten million copies worldwide. It was also the biggest debut album and the biggest album by a female artist in 2002. Only *The Eminem Show* and *Nellyville* sold more copies in that year. Avril was no longer the new kid on the block – she was a genuine rock and roll phenomenon.

CHAPTER 7.

DRESSED UP LIKE
WE'RE SOMETHING ELSE

Avril's look defines her almost as much as her music: despite
being able to afford the very finest designer clothes in the world,
Avril's style is still very much thrift store chic.

Avril is tiny. Standing at only five foot one inch tall, she looks
younger even than her teenage years. It is said she can actually
fit inside the suitcase she takes on the road with her! Her initial
trademark style gimmick was a neck-tie, usually worn with rolled
up sleeves and baggy, three-quarter-length pants. (Cynics
disliked the fact that already Avril's official merchandise
teams were offering 'Avril neck-ties'.)

she can actually fit

She has a navel piercing and three earrings in total, but she does not have any tattoos. She champions grommet belts, mesh baseball caps (often worn back to front) and both chunky silver and leather string or studded wrist bracelets; her nail varnish is usually a shade of black and often chipped like a true tomboy; she wears football shirts she's owned since she was a little girl; she is also often seen in a white, cotton vest, fitted tightly around her small frame; make-up is restricted to lashings of black eye-liner, otherwise it is decidedly conspicuous by its absence. Her hair is straight, uncoloured and at times almost lank.

Footwear is usually one of two brands – Converse ankle-high boots or more recently the classic black eight-hole Dr Martens boot, known as the 1461 – both rock classics. While the Converse shoe found its place in rock history largely due to photographs of Kurt Cobain wearing them (he was in a pair when he committed suicide), the 1461 ties in Avril's style with forty years of rock history – aligning her with bands such as The Clash, The Who, Foo Fighters, Rancid and a host of subcultures such as goths, psychobillies, mods, punks and skins. For one high-profile interview with *Newsweek*, Avril turned up in cut-off plaid bondage pants, steel-toed Doc Martens and a jacket with a button badge that read 'F*** FASHION.'

As with her songwriting, many older people around Avril try to tell her how to look. This is something that usually happens at almost every photoshoot – so much so that Avril never attends one now without her own clothes either already on or a spare set in a rucksack.

inside the suitcase she takes on the road with her!

She has
instantly
become a
fashion
icon for
a whole
generation
of fans

Like most teenage girls, she may display a certain nonchalance about her fashion, but she is in fact acutely aware of what's hot and what's not. 'I'm very careful about my image,' she says. 'I see what's going on out there today, and I'm totally not into glamming up and looking like someone else for the camera . . . [wearing] heels and skanky tops. I'm not a bitch or anything, but I can be a bitch. People want me to look all pretty and sexy for pictures, and it's just not my thing.'

So what influence is Avril having on her legions of fans? Generally, she's viewed in a positive light – after all, she hasn't veered into bad taste like some other stars . . . a certain Britney and Christina spring to mind: sexy schoolgirl outfits or chaps to reveal your backside? Classy.

With Avril, many people immediately felt it was altogether refreshing to see a female pop/rock star dressed like a throwback from grunge's heyday. She was asking to be judged on the quality of her music, not the size of her breasts.

Avril defiantly questions the way female pop stars sell records through sex, their overly raunchy videos, their skimpy clothes and their salacious lyrics – she says simply that she is 'selling music, not sex'. 'I think a lot of girls look at that stuff and it makes them self-conscious because their body doesn't look that good,' she said in an interview with *Rolling Stone*. 'And they don't want their boyfriend staring at that shit. It's just not my thing. I want people to watch my video and not be staring at my girl parts but to be listening to my lyrics and hearing what I have to say and watching me rock out on my guitar.'

At first, she made no secret of her dislike for some pop stars. Britney was first in line, 'I mean, the way she dresses – would you walk around the street in a f***in' bra? I'm not trying to diss anyone, but with me, the clothes I wear onstage are the clothes I would wear to school or go shopping . . . She's not being herself up there because she's dancing like a ho . . . It's definitely not what I'm going to do.'

Avril and her band don't need to be dressed up or styled like other pop stars. They play award ceremonies in the clothes they're wearing on the journey to the show. They walk off the stage and head to the after-show party in the same gear. Sweaty? Maybe.

However, despite being essentially anti-fashion, Avril's impact has been such that she has instantly become a fashion icon for a whole generation of fans. The power of this profile and stylistic influence on young society was shown by a remarkable anecdote concerning her choice of T-shirt when she appeared on the ever-popular late night chat show *Saturday Night Live* in New York in January 2003. On her top half, she donned a small red T-shirt emblazoned with the legend, 'Home Hardware, Napanee'.

Within 60 seconds of her two-song performance on the show (singing 'I'm With You' and 'Complicated'), the answerphone at that hardware shop in her hometown was ringing off the hook. When the proprietors checked in for business at 10 a.m. the next day, the phone continued to ring relentlessly with Avril fans from all over America pleading with them to mail them a similar shirt. The store's manager, Dustin Bee, had had the surprise of his life when settling down the night before to watch *Saturday Night Live*, saying, 'I couldn't believe it at first, took a second look, realized it was Home Hardware, saw the Napanee underneath.' Dustin's father Dale owns the store. The near-eight minutes Avril and his hardware store logo were on screen would have cost him precisely $1,125,000 in advertising fees. Some years before, he had sponsored a team from the Greater Napanee Soccer Association for $175. Now that old shirt and the name of his business were on national television on the chest of the music world's hottest new star, in front of an audience of millions.

In the aftermath of this fabulous series of events, Dale and his son organised a re-issue of the shirts in order to raise funds for the same soccer team he had sponsored all that time ago. Avril was

Multi-national corporations all over the world were offering Avril millions of dollars to endorse their products

delighted to see the chance success her choice of shirt had caused, only adding that it would be nice if all the new T-shirts could be manufactured locally in Napanee in order to benefit the town. One final example of the influence of Avril's style came in August 2002, when the revered Rock 'n' Roll Hall of Fame in Cleveland asked her to lend them the outfit she wore in the video for 'Complicated', to be included in their exhibition of ultra-contemporary artists entitled 'On The Charts'. Rock purists were appalled, pointing out that Avril was hardly part of rock and roll legend with only one, albeit successful, single and a popular debut album behind her. Undeterred, the museum borrowed her white tank top, cargo shorts and trademark neck-tie from that video. She was in good company too, with other exhibits from the likes of Destiny's Child, Rage Against The Machine, Sum 41, Eminem and Madonna.

Avril was bluntly honest about her surprise at the request. 'I think that's ridiculous,' she said, 'because I've had one single out and I'm like this new kid in this music scene. OK, I think it's funny, but at the same time, I'm like, "Hell yeah, I'll give you my clothes!"'

CHAPTER 8.

SLAMMING ON HER GUITAR

If 'Complicated' had been the perfect debut single then Avril's follow-up, 'Sk8er Boi', was a definite signal of future intent. Its rockier guitars and new wave thunder immediately made people sit up and notice that there was much more to her music than radio-friendly pop/rock.

The video was directed by Francis Lawrence and shot in late July 2002 in downtown Los Angeles. It perfectly captures the underground feel of the song, centred as it is around an illegal street gig by Avril. Flyers, graffiti and word of mouth all announce the secret location using a red star - Avril's logo - which is painted on walls, a car and the actual intersection where the gig is to take place. Right on cue, Avril plus about three thousand fans emerge from the back streets to rock out.

As with all her videos, Avril's band is featured throughout the video, but it is the young singer who is the focus of the clip. During filming, the director gave Avril $100 for putting a dead cockroach on her tongue for ten seconds! You go, girl! With the help of this video, Avril's second single was another smash hit, reaching the top ten in charts all over the globe, with a more modest top fifteen placing in the USA. Sales of the album were revitalised too and anticipation for the forthcoming tour dates was reaching fever pitch.

Ironically, considering how much emphasis has been put on Avril's skateboarding antics, she says she is no longer that good. 'I don't get much chance to do it any more [like] when I was in high school,' she says. 'I suck. I like to skate, it's fun, but . . . I like to do it

On stage is where she really comes alive

in my free time. I don't want someone to shove a camera and a board in my face and be like, "Here, let's see what everyone's talking about." Because it's not like I'm a pro.'

The video for 'Sk8er Boi' also showcases Avril's live sound, which couldn't be more different from those other pop princesses. Her shows are simple, straight-to-the-point rock gigs. The raucous guitars and painfully loud volume is often something of a shock for the legions of young fans (invariably dressed in tank tops and ties) who have been happily singing along to the far more polished and amenable sounds on the album. Yet Avril would not have it any other way. On stage is where she really comes alive. 'I really like performing when I'm mad,' she says, 'and I'm always mad at boys.'

Behind her is the band, made up of drummer Matthew Brann, bassist Mark Spicoluk and guitarists Jesse Colburn and Evan Taubenfeld. They tour together, hang out together and are a very tightly knit unit. They appear in her videos and have even started to write songs together – Avril and Evan wrote a track very shortly after their first ever meeting (some of these collaborative efforts are expected on Avril's sophomore album). She has also admitted to 'having a crush on each of them' at some point! Is it love on the tour bus, then?

They're all close in age, being in their late teens or early twenties. Avril says they are all her best friends but she is closest to Evan, the serious and clever one. Matt is the joker in the pack who loves telling anecdotes and tales. Avril describes the blue-haired guitarist Jesse as a 'crazy psycho punk rocker'! He was, after all, formerly in a band called Closet Case, described by one reporter as 'a Canadian anarchist-vegetarian-peace-punk band'!

Contrary to accusations by critics that Avril is already letting her ego get in the way of business, she defiantly praises this band at every opportunity. 'I'm a solo artist and it's my name,' she admits, 'but I have the band vibe and I want people, when they hear my name or think "Avril Lavigne", to think of me and the guys. That's how much I want them to be involved in this. We have something really special and we connect really well. It's strange, but it really feels like we're all supposed to be together. It's a really cool, unique situation.'

In the spring of 2003, Avril headed out on the road for her first full world tour, a daunting series of shows starting in Tacoma and ending twenty-one gigs and three continents later in Brisbane, Australia, with more shows being added along the way due to the huge demand. Here's a girl who isn't afraid to push herself!

Inevitably, the physical and emotional demands of promoting/ touring occasionally took their toll on Avril – after all, in one promotional spell in the winter of 2002, she had been on 35 planes in 28 days, not an ideal scenario for an asthma sufferer. 'Lots of late nights,' she told VH1. 'Flights get in late and by the time you check into your hotel room, unpack your toothbrush, brush your teeth, go to bed . . . and then you have to get up early in the morning – which is what it's been like for me lately – my body's just not used to it and it's getting worn down. So my throat is getting kind of hoarse and raspy. I have a couple of red patches in there now, so I'm [sometimes] on some antibiotics to fix that up. I just have to try to stop talking and screaming and jumping around when I don't really need to.'

The vocal demands are exacerbated by the rocking nature of her gigs. Avril has even been known to cover hard rocking metalheads System of a Down on tour. The Avril Lavigne live act was considered hard enough to be asked to perform at two particularly prestigious events in 2003: the Brit Awards in London and a Metallica tribute concert organised by MTV, also starring Sum 41, Korn and Limp Bizkit. Notably, her first headline US tour was titled The *Try To Shut Me Up* Tour, a title which could perhaps have been a reference to the amazing volume of her band!

In tandem with this fantastic live reputation, Avril has acquired something of a name for being a 'wild child'. She makes no secret of her intention to enjoy life and, as such, has earned this reputation as a pop/rock star who doesn't play by the rules. In interviews she has readily described getting in to bar fights and such tales of excess are invariably littered with descriptive expletives, rather than the sickly 'oh, my gosh' of her more saccharine celeb peers. Even her own website calls her 'a skater-punk, a dynamic spirit, a true wild child'.

In August 2002 she told *Rolling Stone* about one bar fracas in particular. 'The other night, I got into three fights,' she confessed. 'I was at a club and some girl was giving me attitude. When people are drinking, they get mouthy. She pushed me, and I got her down on the floor. Security came, and because I was on top, they threw me out.'

Another example is when she recalled how with a friend she once jumped off a very high bridge without knowing for certain if the water was shallow or contained hidden rocks. 'We were like, "Let's just do it!" We jumped. I screamed and when I hit the water I was like, "I'm alive!"' The girl's going loco!

Of course, many stars like to let the public think they are rather more outrageous than they actually are - it sells records, always has and always will. At least Avril's rebellious streak was clear for everyone to see. One comical example was a night out with fellow Canadian punks Sum 41, whose 'Fat Lip' breakthrough single and subsequent *All Killer No Filler* album, blending old school metal and new generation punk, had catapulted them to global fame. During a tour of smaller venues across North America to promote their sophomore effort, *Does This Look Infected?*, Sum 41's entourage - including their friend Avril - hit a New York bar called Lit to celebrate their gig at the hallowed punk mecca CBGBs. Sum 41 drummer Steve O admitted to downing numerous shots of Jagermeister and tequila, after which vocalist Deryck Whibley pounced on to the bar and pulled his trousers down. Avril quickly jumped up and then tried to pull Deryck's boxer shorts down too! According to Steve O on the band's website, Deryck was 'half-naked and too drunk to do anything about it'.

Steve O, on the other hand, reacted with lightning reflexes to his fellow band mate's predicament. 'I saw the opportunity and grabbed Avril's underpants, lifting her up off the ground, delivering the best wedgie of my career, in front of everyone at the bar.' Cheekily, Avril later denied this was a true version of

events when talking on *Top of the Pops*, saying, 'I was the one who gave Steve a wedgie . . . and I'm gonna get him back large . . . There'll be payback.'

Unlike other female pop stars, Avril has no problem with antics such as this and what people might consequently think of her suitability as a role model. 'It won't really make me change,' she affirms. 'I'm not worried about what other people say. I'm just going to be myself. I'm not going to try to pretend I'm someone else. I'm not a bad person. I like to have fun and I like to be myself. Hopefully, people will see that.'

Yet in contrast to this more controversial streak, Avril says she likes to avoid swearing in her songs so as not to disappoint or embarrass her Christian parents – despite her interviews being littered with profanities. And in another endearing reminder of her youthfulness, Avril further explained, 'Sometimes I am [shy]. Sometimes I get nervous, but then again I can be that wild kid jumping around being the loudest in the room. I mean everyone goes through different emotions. I'm not gonna be hyper 24/7. You don't wanna see me drink Coke, though – I don't shut up! I can't drink coffee or eat chocolate either 'cos I get really loud.'

I'M NOT WORRIED ABOUT WHAT OTHER PEOPLE SAY. I'M JUST GOING TO BE MYSELF

CHAPTER 9.

IN MY WORLD

When such a young star has been catapulted to glittering fame
and fortune, seemingly overnight, there are always many people
keen to criticise. Avril's main detractors expressed how ridiculous
they felt it was that she openly complained about promotional
duties - interviews, photoshoots and so on - even though she had
only been in the industry a few months. They pointed to veterans
like The Rolling Stones, who had been doing such admittedly
banal tasks for nearly forty years. The New York comedy circuit
picked up on this point and one stand-up joker berated Avril's
breakthrough song, 'Complicated', asking, 'How can life be so
complicated? You are only sixteen! Life's like that! Huh, life's like
what? You haven't had any life yet!' For Avril, this was all part of
the job and she had to learn not to take this criticism to heart.

She also has to get used to the dramatic effect her celebrity
status has already had on her day-to-day life. Her parents point
out that she occasionally still goes to her favourite pizzeria when
she is back home in Napanee (La Pizzeria), although instead of
hanging out there with friends from high school like she used to,
she has to have take-out.

I DREAM ABOUT PIZZA

Fans from all over the world have been flocking to Napanee to see where their heroine was brought up

However, it is a well-known fact that dairy produce is not good for singers and Avril, it seems, is prepared to go without. '[Dairy] is bad to for voice and my throat,' she says. 'You know the sacrifice that is for me to live without eating pizza? I dream about pizza.' She hasn't had to change all her eating habits, however. Before she was famous she would often get the munchies in the middle of the night and head off to the nearby 24-hour convenience store for tofu, and she still does to this day.

What about the millions of dollars that have streamed into her bank account since her first flush of success? Her parents happily told *Popworld* magazine how Avril is not in a rush to spend it. While her mother diplomatically says, 'she's always been a saver,' her father is rather more direct, saying, 'She's a tightwad, a mini-Scrooge! A while ago, we went by a BMW place and I said, "You could get a convertible." I was just teasing her but she got so mad and told me, "Dad, I just want to get a used Jeep."'

Avril's personal assistant, Shannon Reddy, can see why the young star might find the financial implications of her success a little daunting. 'She's amazingly grounded. It hasn't seemed to hit her yet. [With money] I think she needs to see something on paper that shows her exactly how much she has.' For her part, she simply says, 'All I know is that I wanna live in a decent house and sleep in a clean bed, I'll be happy.' Anything but ordinary? Hardly.

It isn't just herself and her family that have been impacted by the multimillion-selling success of *Let Go*. Avril's huge international success has also had an unexpected and entirely positive effect on her hometown, which she always talks about fondly in interviews. As a result, fans from all over the world have been flocking to Napanee to see where their heroine was brought up. The local post office/general store – where Avril's mother still collects her papers each day – has been swamped with fan mail addressed simply, 'To: Avril Lavigne, Napanee, Canada.' Sometimes fans even send her skateboards as gifts.

In recognition of this boost to the town's profile and local economy, the councillors of Napanee organised a party at her old school in early 2003 on the night of her Grammy appearance (despite a sign outside the Town Hall reading 'Skateboarding and Rollerblading Prohibited'). In the lead up to the event, Napanee Mayor David Remington was warmly enthusiastic about Avril's contribution to his town, gleefully telling the *Toronto Star* that, 'This is absolutely huge. Everybody in Napanee is extremely proud of her. [Plans to honour Avril] will likely be an ongoing process where we will do whatever is appropriate to honour her in consultation with Avril and her family and managers.'

For now, they revealed an over-sized Christmas card signed by hundreds of local residents, which was later handed over to the Lavigne family. Students at Avril's school also set up a permanent 'hall of fame' of their own to inspire fellow Napanee residents to live their dream. Her contribution to the grander promotion of Canada itself was even brought up in that country's House of Commons, when her constituency MP Larry McCormick said, 'Canadians from sea to sea to sea are cheering for you, Avril. Good luck and God bless as you enter the realm of the stars. Everyone at home is pulling for you, Avril.' Ah, bless.

On an international level, things were not always so rosy. When Avril appeared to make anti-war comments during the American-UK led liberation of Iraq in March 2003, her critics came out even more vociferously. Fortunately for Avril, the public seemed not to take too much offence, unlike the Dixie Chicks, who were soundly berated for making similar anti-war statements. Back in Napanee, none of this mattered when they named her 'Citizen of the Year, 2002'

Avril's family still lives in the same house and she still lives there too, on the few occasions when she is not out of town working. Her jet-set lifestyle has changed things for the Lavignes in many ways. Their daughter has been so busy that even Avril's mother sometimes has difficulty getting in touch – daily phone calls are a ritual but her rock star girl is in so many countries so often that they hardly get chance to actually spend much time together. Avril's miniature schnauzer dog, Sam, like her battered old skateboard, is not able to travel on the road with her much either. Avril also struggles to spend much time with her siblings, instead thanking them in the liner notes for her debut album *Let Go*, saying, 'I know my voice got really annoying to hear 24/7, sorry.' The rock star life doesn't allow for a family.

'I still have my room back home,' she told *ElleGirl* magazine, 'so I guess that's where I live officially, but really I live in different hotels in different cities, out of suitcases. I miss home a lot. I talk to my mom every single day. I really miss my brother and sister. I was home for Christmas and I saw my best friends who are totally psyched about what's happening to me. I also saw my ex-boyfriend, who dumped me for no good reason. That was kinda cool, though, 'cause you gotta wonder if he regrets it now.' What a loser.

This was not the only element of Avril's life that was a million miles from normality. Regarding potential boyfriends, something most girls her age spend all day thinking about, she said, 'I'm not in a relationship and I'm not looking.' That said, a gentleman called Tim Skerpon, appropriately a skater boy, was rumoured to be seeing her. Whether she will ever be able to find someone she is certain wants to be with her for herself, not her money or fame, is another matter. This is a dilemma that troubles many celebrities who are not in a serious relationship when they get their big break. That said, Avril is so busy promoting her first album and working on her new record that even if she did have a boyfriend, she would barely have time to see him!

Avril also admits to being drawn to some of these more 'ordinary' attractions in life. 'When I pass a wedding dress I freak out. I already have my dress picked out in my head. I am going to be really poufy. Oh my god – I just can't wait. I have so much to look forward to – falling in love, getting married, having a nice house and a family. But that is a while . . .'

CHAPTER 10.

PERFECT POWER PUNK POP PIXIE PRINCESS. OR NOT

By the early summer of 2003, Avril was a huge global star. Yet there were still those who suggested she was just a manufactured lightweight punk/pop princess, despite all her angry protestations to the contrary. Fortunately, Avril had the ideal riposte up her sleeve in the form of her next single, 'I'm With You'. In the photographer-turned-director David LaChapelle video for the single (shot in LA), she is seen in a bar/nightclub, isolated from the rest of the crowd by ingenious cinematography which illuminates her sense of emotional detachment. The viewer can't help but feel sorry for the miniscule Avril, bumped and knocked around the bustling club or standing in a freezing, windswept street. At times, she appears so lost and tiny that it seems only her chunky Doc Martens are anchoring her down and stopping her from blowing away in the breeze.

A lush, addictive and emotional song that craftily realigned Avril's image far away from the sugary pop corner of the music world. 'I'm With You' is undoubtedly Avril's most important song to date. Not only does it make fans, radio programmers and critics readdress their preconceptions of her music, but it also beautifully primes people's inquisitiveness in preparation for the follow-up album to Let Go.

It was yet another smash single, hitting number seven in the UK and eventually number four in the USA, as well as similar chart positions all over the world. In the UK in particular, the song had a remarkable effect on the chart life of *Let Go*, sales of which were fuelled sufficiently to see it climb back up to the top spot in March 2003. While other pop artists usually see their albums chart high and then sink without trace within a few weeks, Avril had now been lodged in the album lists around the globe for months. By the time she dives back into the studio for her second album, it is likely that *Let Go* will have been in the UK and US charts for over a year.

'I'm With You' was also important in realigning Avril's media image. Her success has seen her labelled with various tags by a media hungry for a new sensation. The most popular phrase has been that of the 'anti-Britney', a punk princess or, worse still, a 'pixie-punk'. This is not just about the aforementioned stylistic differences between herself and more manicured pop rivals. It is equally about attitudes to life. Avril couldn't be less like a super-celebrity, styled to within an inch of her life, dressed up in designer clothes and bling-bling jewellery, that's a million miles from the ordinary fan on the street. By way of a small but indicative example, while Britney thanks God on MTV bedecked in multi-carat diamonds, Avril chews gum and pulls it out of her mouth on TRL. She has far more in common with the errant and alternative mentality of songwriter/performer Pink than with the likes of Britney Spears and Mandy Moore. Avril and Pink are just like ordinary girls.

Avril is also at the forefront of the rock-versus-pop argument that dominated music in 2003. She is often outspoken about this – at one gig in Orlando, it was reported that she openly mocked the pop acts sharing the bill, Aaron Carter and O-Town, which got her roundly booed by the crowd. On hearing these heckles, Avril started to swear and was promptly cut off by the sound engineers. *American Idol* judge and all-round hate figure for much of the USA, Simon Cowell, came out heavily on Avril's side in this argument, saying that at least she was 'real'. Good man.

I'M NOT PUNK. I NEVER SAID I WAS PUNK. AND MY MUSIC IS DEFINITELY NOT PUNK

Yet despite this controversial stance, she distances herself from even the simplest of tags. 'I'm being labelled as punk, and punk is so not commercial. I'm not punk. I never said I was punk. And my music is definitely not punk.' She sees herself now as more of 'a rock-pop person'.

The biggest question for Avril is whether such enormous success and growing credibility could be maintained. Although at first she seemed quite nonchalant to her astonishing success, gradually the enormity of her impact began to dawn on her. 'It does get overwhelming,' she admits. 'I'm just starting to realise that. I was fine a little while ago but now that things are taking off that's when the stress is coming in, the crazy lifestyle. It's not a normal thing for a seventeen-year-old to be going through.' Too right.

All eyes were now turning towards the second album. According to Avril, this record will be much louder! 'The music I listen to is hard, and the next record will definitely be a heavier rock record. *Let Go* is a lot more polished than I wanted it to be. It's OK, though, because looking at it from a business point of view, it helped me break.' With Arista now fully behind her rockier sound and the question of who writes the songs long since resolved, Avril is hoping that the recording of this follow-up album will be much quicker than the rather protracted *Let Go* sessions.

That difficult second album may not be such a chore because, Avril says, 'I write all the time. That's how I deal with my feelings and emotions. If all of this came to an end, I would still write and sit down with my laptop and work on my songs. It's really important to me and I'm really excited about my second record.'

There were rumours of a collaboration with Fred Durst of Limp Bizkit. Early impressions from whispers in and around Avril's studio sessions suggested the second album was getting heavier and heavier as it progressed. Will her fans follow her down a rocky road? One thing is for certain, by the time of its eventual release, the anticipation and advance interest in Avril's second album will be massive.

EPILOGUE: NO MORE THE CHICKEN-FRIED ASS

Avril Lavigne arrived in 2002 as a breath of fresh air in a staid and repetitive music world. She immediately won over millions of fans with her infectious music, appealing style and outspoken honesty about life, love and music. Equally, she infuriates scores of critics and members of the public who find her brash views and opinionated directness a little hard to handle. She rocks on stage and parties off it, swears liberally and yet writes poignantly. Brazenly ambitious yet conversely indifferent to so many of the clichéd rock star ideals, she is an inspiration to a generation of young girls, more than a few young men and a not insubstantial number of (albeit more secretive) older rockers. She has made the self-indulgent excesses and creative under-achievements of the recent arrogant pop years look out-dated and old-fashioned and in the process set a new benchmark for teenage music by which future aspiring stars will undoubtedly be measured. For all these reasons, she is perhaps the most vibrant and essential new artist of the third millennium.

For all the lofty reviews and record-breaking sales figures, Avril's own take on her new life as a celebrity remains unchanged. Far from assuming that her future career is guaranteed, Ms Lavigne displays an admirable sense of perspective about her new ambitions now that her goal of becoming a rock star has been fulfilled. 'I am hoping I don't disappear too fast and never have to think of something else to do.'

It looks like this is one girl who's here to stay.

AVRIL TRIVIA

Birthday: 27 September 1984
Star Sign: Libra
Hometown: Napanee, Ontario, Canada
Shoe size: 7
Height: 5'1"
Hair Colour: Blonde
Eye Colour: Blue-Green
Favourites:
Colours: black or red
Pizza Toppings: Olives
Clothes: Dickies, Osiris shoes
Oddest Skill: She can bite her own toes.
Favourite Cosmetics: Avril uses Roc moisturizer
and MAC nail polish.

Avril's middle name is shrouded in secrecy because she doesn't like it — most bets are on Ramona.

If Avril wasn't a rock star, she'd like to be a cop, because it is a job with 'great emotions and danger'.

Avril says she carries only one suitcase while on the road, which contains: five pairs of pants, seven T-shirts, two sweaters, one coat, a few pairs of shoes, a Chapstick and some MAC nail polish in her trademark shade of black.

Avril claims she washes her hair only once a week, using random samples of shampoos from hotels. She wears eyeliner, mascara and a bit of shadow but refuses lipstick, foundation, powder or blush. Her hair is kept straight with an anti-frizz product, although one rumour suggests she actually uses mayonnaise!

When MuchMusic offered the chance to meet Avril in person as a competition prize, over 5,000 fans turned up.

Avril uses a camouflage lunchbox for her purse.

In November 2002 Avril became a character in the computer game The Sims, alongside Beyoncé Knowles, LL Cool J and Ludacris, who were all appearing in exclusive scenes available only on AOL.

In late 2002, a computer virus called 'Lirva' (Avril backwards) afflicted machines in 107 Countries.

If she could write her own entry in a musical encyclopaedia, Avril would say, 'Young-spirited Energizer battery bunny'.

Avril has since been playing drums part-time for years.

Backstreet Boy Nick Carter asked Avril to sing on his solo album but she declined, saying, 'It's not really my thing.' Justin Timberlake has said he would love to tour with her and British cheeky chappie Robbie Williams has made it known he wants to duet with the young rocker.